LETTERS,

&c.

LETTERS

TO

LORD ALTHORP,

CHANCELLOR OF THE EXCHEQUER, &c.

ON HIS

PROPOSED CHANGE OF THE TITHE SYSTEM,

THE

WORKING OF THE POOR LAWS;

WITH

PLAN OF EXTENSIVE RELIEF FOR THE

LANDED INTEREST.

LONDON:

J. HATCHARD AND SON, 187, PICCADILLY.

1833.

LONDON:

IBOTSON AND PALMER, PRINTERS, SAVOY STREET, STRAND.

LETTERS.

LETTER I.

ON THE TITHE SYSTEM.

My Lord,

When your Lordship is reported to have stated in your speech, on moving for leave to bring in a bill for the " Commutation of Tithes," that the "occupiers of the soil would have this advantage, that they would be enabled to employ their capital in the cultivation and improvement of the land, without being checked by the payment of tithes, as under the present system," the public would be led to suppose that the occupiers of the land were actually suffering from the pressure of the present mode of collecting them. Similar observations have also been made by owners of estates, anxious to court popularity, and to be liberal at their neighbour's expense, that it is a great hardship,

B

that an increased demand for tithes should be made, where capital has been expended in improvements upon the land. Members of parliament have also addressed their constituents to the same effect, and have told them, the present mode of taking tithes operates as an unjust tax on the capital and skill of the agriculturalist; and they put forward the case of a yeoman, taking a farm that is run out upon a lease of twenty-one years, and upon which it is necessary to expend a considerable capital; and before he receives a shilling of benefit for the money he has laid out, and the skill he has employed, the tithe man steps in, and takes away a portion of that capital, to which he is not in equity entitled.

It might be supposed from the tenor of such observations, that a farmer is a dull, heavy being, and on taking a lease of fourteen or twenty-one years, is so blind to his own interests, that he always makes a most improvident bargain with his landlord. But experience shows that the farmer is not ignorant of the ways of the world —he has not attended towns on market-days without deriving some experimental knowledge; and I would appeal to your Lordship, whether, in all your experience, amidst all your inquiries about long horns and short horns, you ever heard of a farmer returning from the fair, like Moses, in the Vicar of Wakefield, with a gross of green spectacles in payment for the horse he had parted with. The farmer, in these days, is an active-minded man, and fully alive to his own interests; he does not sit idle with his hands before him, or allow his landlord to fix his rent, without making a few observations upon the tithes and the poor-rates.

As a practical example is better than a hundred theoretical cases, I will mention an instance of hiring a farm, which took place in a maritime county, where the land and the advowson of the living belonged to the same proprietor. The mode in which the farmer proceeded to hire his land was this: he commenced, as all good husbands ought to do, with consulting his wife, and the following dialogue passed between them:—"There is an excellent farm to be hired in the neighbourhood, that John Dobbins, who drank so hard, used to occupy, that is very much run out. I have looked it over, and find, upon laying out a certain capital, I shall receive good interest for my money, and get the whole of it back at the end of my lease, with a considerable addition, which will enable us to retire and live comfortably upon our means. You know me too well to suppose I would lay out ten pounds upon another man's land, without the certainty of being re-

paid with interest, however short the time
might be I hired it for." The good woman re-
plies, " I can have no possible objection; you
are too 'cute not to know well what you are
about; only take care to make the best bargain
you can with the parson and the squire."—
" Don't trouble your head about that, mistress,
leave that to me; you know how I persuaded
the owner of the homestead and land we now
occupy, that I did him a favour to cultivate it,
and there is no fear but I shall succeed here."

Before he proceeds to the Hall, he, according
to the understanding which subsists amongst
farmers, had induced some two or three, who
had no intention of hiring the land, to look
over it, and who would afterwards report their
various opinions to the squire: one says the
land is so completely run out, he would not
rent it at half-a-crown an acre; another, he
would not have it, if he was obliged to cultivate it; a third, that the buildings were so
much dilapidated and out of repair, that he
must altogether decline having any thing to do
with it. The owner, who had lost two years'
rent by his former bad tenant, feels much
vexed and annoyed by these observations, and
begins to fear he shall not secure an occupier
for his land upon any terms. Our friend, the
farmer, who really had serious intentions of be-

coming a tenant, at last presents himself, and commences operations with observing, he had heard a great many persons had been to look at the land, but that it was in so bad a state, they would have nothing to say to it, and assures him, should he take the farm, he must lay out a large sum of money in improvements —that a large capital was required to bring it into a proper state of cultivation, and after all, when he had done this, the parson would step in, and deprive him of the fruits of his industry and capital, by taking his tithes in kind. After a long discussion, the farmer carried his point, and secured a lease of the land for twenty-one years, at a rent considerably under its fair and proper value. His next step was to see the clergyman upon the subject of a composition in lieu of tithes. He took care, however, to omit the circumstance which told so well before with his landlord, that he intended to lay out a considerable sum in improving the land, and assured the rector, the owner of the property considered it to be in so bad a state, that he had only fixed a very low rent upon it, to prevent its entirely going out of cultivation. The conference ended in the farmer's agreeing to pay a small composition in lieu of tithes during his term, and he returned home well satisfied with his day's work; and this artless, unsophisticated being retires to his pillow with the reflection that his knowledge of the ways of the world had enabled him to outwit the squire, and to make an easy victim of the parson.

The squire, after a short time, felt much dissatisfied at the low rent he had obtained, and complained it was hard and unjust that so heavy a burden as tithe should be laid upon the land; that he had been able to obtain a very inadequate rent for a farm of his own, owing to this very circumstance. To add to his mortification, he finds the farmer growing rich, his son able to keep his hunter, the daughter sent to a boarding school, and, to crown all, the farmer and his family live upon the best terms with the rector, who, far from being vexed at receiving a small composition for his tithes, is delighted with the cheerful smiles of his parishioners, and in witnessing the high state of cultivation and improved condition of the country.

At last the eyes of the squire were completely opened, and he discovers so large a capital was not required to improve the land as had been previously represented to him, and too late found out that he had made a most improvident bargain.

After some consideration and reflection, a sudden and extraordinary change takes place in his opinions, and he brings forward a string of arguments in defence of the very system he had before found fault with.

"It never occurred to me," he exclaimed, "at the time I made use of such strong language against the tithe system, that I was patron of the living, as well as owner of the land ; my son, for whom I purchased it, has made the army his profession, and it is now worth six thousand pounds. I am resolved how to act. I will advertise the next presentation, and am determined, although I cannot go into the church, yet I will get something out of the church. I have been hasty in laying the blame upon the clergyman, who is as much entitled to receive his tithes, as I am to sell them. The same arguments which might be made use of to abolish tithes would act with still greater force against the payment of my rents. Why should I be deprived of the full value of my living? it is true, I only paid one thousand pounds for it, but it is now worth six times that sum, in consequence of the capital which has been laid out by the spirited farmers who have occupied the land." The living is advertised in the flowery language of a fashionable auctioneer, as a parish "where the luxuriant crops of the by-gone season demonstrate, in terms by no means equivocal, the general superiority of the soil—where the farmers are spirited and wealthy, and the words abatement or postponement of the payment of tithes, is not to be found in their vocabulary." The paragraph catches the eye of the public, and he meets with a purchaser at the price of six thousand pounds, and thus at once secures to himself and heirs three hundred pounds per annum, without any duty to perform, or without incurring the smallest share of responsibility.

It is thus evident the occupiers of land have no reason to complain of the payment of tithes being a hardship, because they always hire the land, taking into consideration the amount of poor-rates and tithes charged upon them, and the capital they may think proper to expend for increasing the productiveness of the soil. Still less have landlords, who are patrons of livings, reason to feel dissatisfied, when, by the sale of their presentations and advowsons, they are enabled to acquire and keep in their own possession more than half of the profits of the tithes.

After reading this statement, we can imagine the people with one voice exclaiming, how advantageous to the country it would be, could any means be devised for placing a large portion of the patronage of the church in the hands of permanent constituted bodies, who would prevent the laity appropriating to themselves a great part of those revenues which were originally set apart by the piety of good men for the support of the members of the church. And, thanks to the wisdom of our forefathers, the way has not only been discovered, but is at this very time in full and active operation. The advowsons of above three thousand benefices being vested in the crown, archbishops, bishops, deans, and chapters, and our two universities, the country possesses a strong and safe guarantee that these cannot be made the subject of bargain and sale, and that the patronage of them will be honourably and beneficially exercised. Even the whisper of censure has not yet been heard against the pure mode in which the presentations in the gift of the crown have been disposed of; and it is affirmed, without fear of contradiction, the preferment in the hands of the ecclesiastical bodies we have named, to have been equally well and conscientiously administered. It is these venerable bodies which give a high character to the Church of England, and the welfare of the people themselves requires them to be supported and maintained.

The king upon his throne, as head of the church, with the archbishops, bishops, deans, and chapters, form an ecclesiastical corporation; and the levelling spirits of the age, who are endeavouring to destroy the body, cannot accomplish this purpose without at the same time striking off the head. The destructives of the day are already loud in their exclamations against the large baronial possessions and princely properties of many of our noble peers. They tell us the arguments they bring forward against the clergy for enjoying small incomes for performing certain duties, may be applied with much greater force to themselves, who form the idle part of the community, and hold their great estates subject to no conditions. Should these noble persons disregard the benefits which the people receive from our venerable institutions, at least for their own sakes and their own order, they ought not to volunteer to lead on the forlorn hope in the attacks upon the property of the church, which forms, as it were, the key-stone of their own. They may rest assured, when this is once loosened and gives way, the mitre, the coronet, and the crown, will be hurled from the heads of their possessors, and will be buried in one indiscriminate and common ruin.

I entreat the legislature, before it listens to the cry of desperate agitators, and proceeds with a rash hand to deprive the clergy of the half portion of the tithes, which in so many cases they only possess, the other half being enjoyed by the laity, to ponder well these words, which ought to be written in letters of gold, " Strike, but hear."

I am, my Lord, your's, &c.

E. N.

LETTER II.

ON TITHES.

My Lord,

As it is an admitted principle, that the government of a country has no right to the obedience, nor the crown any claim to the allegiance, of the people, except it afford protection to their property, I therefore confidently hope, in the consideration of the Tithe Commutation Bill, a fraud upon the clergy, or the confiscation of the revenues of the church, is not intended; and that the subject will be approached with calmness and deliberation.

And it is more particularly the duty of those who shall have voices in deciding this question, to be upon their guard; because erroneous statements have been put forth by those whose duty ought to have led them to make accurate inquiries on the subject. The King's speech had prepared the way for the introduction of this measure, when it informed us, that "the complaints which have been made from the collection of tithes require another system."

At first sight it will be evident, that this statement made by his Majesty's ministers is founded in error; for although some persons may be found who consider the tithe system to have defects, and require alteration, still the causes which are assigned for the complaints against it, do not exist; and for this plain reason, " tithes have not been collected in kind."

We do not mean to assert that some parishes out of above ten thousand, have not paid tithes in kind; in some few instances this might have been done; but this is so far from militating against our statement, that it goes a long way to confirm it. In a word, it is admitted throughout the country, that tithes are compounded for; the collection of tithes in kind forms an exception to the rule. Other causes then must be sought for, which have produced the clamour and raised the cry against the tithe system.

And, in the first place, we attribute it to the landlords, who have stood in the foremost rank, ready to rush forward and seize the tempting spoil—men who have shut their eyes to the

fact, that their own interests are closely inter-
woven with the system they have been anxious
to abolish; that even should they succeed in
destroying this part of the fabric, will find
themselves buried in its ruins. It is a melan-
choly truth, that a mistaken notion of self-
interest should have confounded the principles
of justice in their minds, and that the de-
pression of their rents should have made them
anxious to appropriate to themselves that part
of the produce of the soil which never belonged
to them, and which has been the property of
the church for so many centuries. If such an
attack had been made on the high rents and
large possessions of the landed interest, we
should have heard it loudly denounced, as an
infamous attempt at robbery and spoliation.
The misfortune is, there is nothing so common,
as for mankind, from wishing a thing to be
true, little by little to bring themselves to be-
lieve it to be so.

It will not be necessary to pursue the subject
further. Landlords are now fully alive to the
mistaken and erroneous line of policy they have
pursued. Political agitators have held up to
their faces a mirror, in which they see an
Agrarian law reflected. They have been told
they hold their lands merely as stewards, for
the use and benefit of the people; and at the

eleventh hour have discovered the arguments they brought forward for the abolition of tithes would be used by the destructives of the day, with a thousand times greater force, for the abolition of their rents.

Then come the farmers, who have been parties to the cry, and have assigned the hardship of the tithe system as a reason for the nonpayment of their rents. They are, however, by far too shrewd a race to be sufferers by the system. They are not, it is to be confessed, political economists; they do not examine whether tithes are a tax upon the gross produce of the land, and fall upon the consumer, or whether they appear in the shape of a rent charge or any other charge; they have not even heard of the " incidence of tithes." They care little whether Ricardo be right or Adam Smith wrong—whether Senior or M'Culloch agree or differ in their first principles of political economy: what they look to are practical measures; and in hiring their lands, they know it to be their interest to play off the landlord against the parson, and the parson against the landlord; and always contrive to have their rents and tithes considerably under their real value.

The farmers occasionally induce the labourers to join in the cry, by telling them they could afford to give higher wages, were the burden of tithes removed from the land; but as they are fully aware, at the time they are making this statement, that it has no foundation in truth, and that it is a mere cloak for their own illiberality, it will not require further notice.

Another party remains to be considered—we mean the conductors of the daily press, who make the abolition of tithes a lever by which they may raise, not the interests of the country, but the sale of their papers. The truth must be spoken—it is with them not so much the abolition of tithes, as the circulation of newspapers. Kind souls! they are willing, for the paltry sum of ten or fifteen thousand a year paid to each proprietor, to ease the public of the trouble of thinking for themselves; and in this manner half a dozen persons, whose opinions, were they to mix in society, would have no weight, and indeed would scarcely be regarded, are enabled to direct the public feeling. They inoculate their wild notions upon the inhabitants of the metropolis, the mass then soon becomes inflamed, and the whole community is infected. They are fully aware the public mind must be excited, or the sale of newspapers must be diminished. The strongest language is therefore used; and, as in the days of Robespierre and the French revolution, they tell us, " tithes have ceased to exist, the public wills them to be abolished."

This appears high-sounding language, and rather startling to timid natures; we will therefore see how this public opinion, as it is called, is brought into action. We would necessarily suppose that it took its rise from the statements of some of our great senators, expressed after the maturest consideration upon the subject. We inquire what great mind has directed its energies to the question? Alas! there is no great mind employed in the case; we return as much dissatisfied with our inquiry, as we were a short time since, when upon looking at the index of one of our great law authorities, we saw " great mind," and opposite, " see judge;" our curiosity was still further excited, and we impatiently turned to the page, to read the treasures of knowledge and wisdom from the stores of the luminous mind of our highly gifted Chancellor; but great was our dismay, when instead of these treasures of wisdom and knowledge being opened to us, we only found " the Chancellor had a great mind to commit the prisoner."

We will give up, then, our notion of great minds being engaged in the consideration of such questions, and will point out the way by which the public is excited on all the leading topics of the day. We must request you to accompany us into a small back room in the Strand, where we shall introduce you to these caterers of the public appetite, with all their cooking apparatus before them—men who calculate to a *turn*, what articles will increase the sale of their papers, and procure them a greater share of emolument. Certain high-seasoned materials are placed before them, out of which they undertake to furnish two courses and a dessert, to satisfy in some measure the voracious appetite of the public. Observe the skill and tact displayed on the occasion. The editor begins with serving up as his leading article, or top dish, the abolition of tithes, which he brings up reeking hot from the Dissenter's oven. The public at first devour it most voraciously; but the ingredients of which it is composed being unwholesome and injurious to the *constitution*, a nausea is created, and they turn with disgust from the feast. The next day, ballot is introduced as the top dish, whilst the abolition of tithes, seasoned with church reform, is removed as a hash to the corner. The public, like all other gourmands, pant for variety, and dishes from Belgium, France, and Holland, are served up in turn. A few light puffs, frothed up with the praises of the administration, are handed round, tasted, and set aside, not possessing the slightest good qualities, and the *trash* is voted out, by general acclamation. Still they are not at a loss, and prove they have studied the appetites of their masters, by having in reserve, ready to be served up hot and hot, in the good old English style, the Bank charter, the East India monopoly, and the slave trade. Turkey is brought forward, an Irish stew is not forgotten, whilst O'Connel, warmed by his eloquence and blackened by his politics, is grilled upon the gridiron, lent for that purpose by the friendly hand of Cobbet; and the banquet ends by his being served up after the most approved fashion of his countrymen, with a *potatoe* in his *head*, and a repeal of the union in his *hand*. Thus they ring their changes, and, like the heroes of the belfry, glory in the sensation produced on the public by their tremendous peal of treble bob majors. And is it, my Lord, from such polluted sources, from such tyrant journalists, that you draw arguments for praising the tri-coloured flag, which the destructives of the day pant for an opportunity to wave over the ruined institutions of your country.

We trust, after this exposure of the arts by which the public have been misled, that our legislators will take the trouble of judging and thinking for themselves, when the important questions relating to the commutation of tithes, and the Church of England Reform measure, come before them.

As Englishmen, we expect all who are called upon to legislate on these important questions, to weigh well the arguments which may be brought forward—not to turn to the right hand or to the left for the sake of courting a little fleeting popularity, which in a moment may be scattered to the winds. We place too firm a reliance on the wisdom and honour of our legislators, to suppose for one moment they are inclined to sacrifice the tithe system, or to make a victim of the church — that they wish to throw the establishment overboard, as a tub for the whale, merely to stop the mouths of the desperate agitators and political unionists of the day. Be not, as land-owners, parties to the suicidal act, which will destroy your own properties. The clergy may be compared to faithful centinels, standing on an eminence, and ever watchful over the best interests of the country; and should they be removed, and the pittance which is now grudgingly yielded, be done away, the attack will be renewed with redoubled fierceness upon the properties of our nobility, who enjoy their tend and twenty thousands a year; and we cannot shut our eyes to the fact, that no confiscations of one description of property can take place, without striking a blow at every other. An Agrarian law would soon eat its way into the heart of the empire, which would be immediately followed by the ruin of this once happy, but now deluded people.

The roar of the multitude, heard above the storm, speaks in terms too intelligible not to be understood, that the downfall of the church would soon be followed by that of the peerage and the monarchy, whilst the signs of the times, like the " hand-writing on the wall," fills us with the direst presages. The words are awful, " God hath numbered thy kingdom, and finished it. Thou art weighed in the balances, and found wanting. Thy kingdom is divided, and given to the Medes and Persians."

May our revered monarch, who, as head of the church, has sworn at his coronation, before the altar of his God, and in the face of his people, " to the utmost of his power to maintain unto the bishops and clergy of this realm, and to the churches committed to their charge, all such rights and privileges as by law do or shall appertain unto them ;"—may the king, I say, reflect upon the awful solemnity of this oath. Should any misgivings arise in the royal mind, let him look to the example and constancy of King Charles the Martyr, whose firmness of resolution made him one of the noblest defenders of the church ; *I will consent to no more, said the king, than reason, justice, honour, and religion persuade me to be for God's glory, the church's good, my people's welfare, and my own peace.*" He singly and alone was obliged to bear the burden and heat of the day, and to stand the foremost in the battle, whilst he eloquently pleaded for the laws of the land, the doctrine and discipline of the church, and for the unalienable revenues of the clergy.

May the affectionate care which he expressed for the welfare of the church descend as an inheritance upon his successors, and rest upon the monarch who now fills the throne. May the strict and solemn charge the royal martyr gave his son, have its due weight in these our days. " *I command you, upon my blessing,*" said the king, " *to be constant to your religion, neither hearkening to Roman superstition, nor the seditious and schismatical doctrines of the presbyterians and independents ; for know that a persecuted church is not thereby less pure, though less fortunate. I command you, upon my blessing, never to yield to any conditions that are dishonourable, though it were for the saving of my life. Above all, I would have you well grounded and settled in your religion, the best profession of which I have ever esteemed that of the Church of England. In this I charge you to persevere, as coming nearest to God's word for doctrine, and to the primitive examples for govern-*

ment. I hope," the monarch further says, "*God will give me and you that grace which will enable us to want as well as wear a crown, which is not worth taking up or enjoying upon sordid, dishonourable, and irreligious terms. Keep you to the true principles of piety, virtue, and honour, and you shall never want a kingdom.*

I am, my Lord, your's, &c.

E. N.

LETTER III.

ON THE WORKING OF THE POOR-LAWS,

WITH A PLAN

FOR THE RELIEF OF THE LANDED INTEREST.

MY LORD,

Although a difference of opinion exists respecting the ability you possess for filling the high office of Chancellor of the Exchequer, your opponents, on the one hand, affirming you have given no proof of talent in your official character, whilst your friends, on the other, contend that it is the invincible modesty of your nature that so effectually conceals it from the public view. However this may be, both friends and foes agree in one particular, that you feel the warmest interest in the welfare of the labouring and agricultural classes. I shall, therefore, submit to your attention a few observations on the present system of the poor-laws, and the remedy by which I conceive the landed interest would be relieved from the burden which now presses so heavily upon it; trusting, if it meets with your approval, you will be induced to bring forward some legislative measure on the subject.

It will not be necessary to enter into a detailed statement to prove that the poor-laws, as they at present exist, proceed with overwhelming force to swallow up nearly the whole profits of the land, and tend to produce an Agrarian law, with this additional evil annexed to it, that it will be forced upon an idle, profligate, and demoralized population. The working of the present system of poor laws in agricultural parishes, where a superabundant population exists, offers as high wages to the idle as can be obtained by the hard-working labourer, who toils from sun-rise to sun-set; in short, it is a premium upon idleness and beggary, by absolutely refusing employment to those who are known to possess the smallest means. The industrious labourer, who has lived under good masters, and at the age of forty, by the most frugal habits, has saved fifty pounds, and is in possession of a comfortably furnished cottage, will, in the event of such master having no further occasion for his services, find no employment in a parish so circumstanced. The farmer will say, I know your character stands high as a good able-bodied workman, and I should be glad to employ you, were I not compelled by the existing laws to pay more labourers than I actually want to cultivate the land. The hardworking man, finding his character for industry of no service to him, and seeing that even the idle and profligate are preferred before him, thus begins to argue. " No one will employ me whilst I possess this little property, the fruit of my hard earnings. I find the only chance I have to procure work, is to part with it all. I must put myself on a level with the diggers in the gravel-pits, I must reduce myself to a state of destitution before any one will employ me." This is not an imaginary case, and many similar ones may be found in the reports of the Commissioners appointed to inquire into the operation of the poor-laws.

In the parish of B., near the coast, in the county of Suffolk, several labourers find employment, during the summer months, in the fisheries, and should they be fortunate enough to earn ten pounds each, they would have no inducement to put it by for a rainy day, as they are too good lawyers not to know that the parish must support them as soon as it is spent; nay, they have every inducement to get rid of it as fast as possible, because the parish officers will not employ them whilst any part of their savings remain; thus they become improvident and reckless for the future. It is true that a labour rate has been established in this as well as in several other parishes, but even if it were to succeed according to the wishes of its warmest advocates, it would not afford any permanent relief, but would only have the effect of perpetuating an increased burden upon the land. I am aware it may be urged in defence of the present system, that the utmost vigilance is exerted by the overseers and by persons appointed to see the laws carried into execution; but the truth is, the blame does not apply to the mode in which the laws are administered, but to the system itself—to that system which offers a premium on idleness and beggary.

By the statute 33rd of Elizabeth, it was intended that assistance should be afforded only 'to the aged, the helpless, and infirm; it never could have been foreseen the time would arrive when able-bodied labourers would claim relief under it, or there would be such a redundancy of labourers that they would not be able to find employment upon the land. That this is actually the fact will appear by looking at the state of the parish we have alluded to, and we find in a population consisting of five hundred and eighty persons, there are thirty agricultural labourers more than the most experienced and intelligent farmers consider requisite for the proper cultivation of the lands. Of course the support of the labourers must create an enormous tax upon the proprietors of these estates. We may fairly reckon ten shillings a week would be paid to each labourer, which, taking the number at thirty, would amount annually to the sum of seven hundred and eighty pounds, or what would be equivalent to it, would require eight hundred acres of the best land in the parish should be set apart for the support of persons who can give no adequate labour in return. This state of the agricultural interest is most alarming; ruin stares the farmer in the face, and the prospect under the present system is, that in a short time landlords will not merely hold their land as trustees for the poor, but they will be obliged, in addition, to find capital to keep it in cultivation.

The only remedy to stop this great and growing evil, is for the legislature to enact an emigration law, a law which is now imperatively called for by the general state of the population of the country. I do not mean that plan of emigration which has been submitted to individuals in some agricultural districts, and where a few persons have been induced to accept the offers made to them. To render it effective, the legislature must form an extensive plan of emigration; government must take this important affair into their own hands; it must, in short, be made a national concern. In this business, my Lord, there is no room for trifling or delay—whilst yourself and colleagues with the sluggard cry out, " Yet a little more sleep, yet a little more slumber," the industrious part of the agricultural population is fast slipping from us, acted upon by the mischievous system of the poor-laws.

Awake, then, O ministers, from your slumbers—arise from your bed of roses—shake off this fatal lethargy—set your house in order, and before you depart, apply the whole energies of government to this important work. Be assured the wretched condition of our labouring population calls loudly upon the legislature for its prompt and immediate attention.

1st. To accomplish this desirable object, I would propose in the first place, that an emigration tax should be laid upon all property, including funded property, which would amount, upon a very small scale, to the sum of *two* or *three* hundred thousand pounds per annum.

2nd. As the interests of the country always require a large naval force to be kept up, even in time of peace, such force might be employed in conveying emigrants to our colonies, which would produce a saving in the charge of freight, to the amount of three hundred thousand pounds per annum.

3rd. By appropriating half a million, from the eight millions at present collected by the poor's rates, to assist the object of emigration.

From his tax, and by appropriating a portion of the eight millions raised by the poor's rates, a sufficient sum would be collected to carry into effect a general emigration of agricultural labourers, who cannot get employment in this country.

A bounty might also be offered to induce labourers to come forward, and assist in promoting the system of emigration; and it is impossible to conceive that the national resources can be applied to better purposes, than in converting the idle, unemployed pauper into a contented and well-disposed labourer. By this system of colonization, one hundred thousand men, who have no means of supporting themselves, with a certain number of women and children, might annually be sent from this country; and as the parishes in the kingdom amount to about ten thousand, each parish, according to circumstances, might be relieved of its proportion of surplus pauper labourers.

It may be objected, that it will be impossible to procure the consent of so many individuals. I answer, that as the poor-laws now in existence tend to discourage industry, and to take the idle and dissolute under their especial protection, so the emigration laws ought at once to have the effect of convincing the idle able-bodied labourers, that they will no longer be upheld by the present defective system. As the working of the poor-laws acts as a heavy weight to depress the industrious labourer, so the emigration law would act as a lever to raise him again to his proper standard in society. The answer which the unmarried labourer now frequently gives to the parish officer is, " Either allow me a larger weekly sum, or I will marry, and then you will have, in addition, my wife and family to maintain." To prevent the idle and dissolute availing themselves of these excuses, a compulsory clause might be inserted in any emigration act, rendering all persons subject to that law, (except those labouring under infirmities, old age, illness, &c. &c.) who may have received parochial relief for a certain period, say three, or five, or seven years. By these means, and by providing for the comforts of emigrants on their arrival at the colonies in every possible way, the proper object of the poor-laws might be obtained, namely, securing relief for the really necessitous and distressed.

Should it be urged, that such a legislative enactment would be an infringement upon the liberties of the people, I admit it would be so to a certain extent—it would take away from the unemployed labourers the liberty of becoming nightly depradators, in search of game —the liberty of rendering themselves wretched; —it would deprive them of the liberty of making themselves outcasts from society, and often save them from suffering the last penalty of the law.

As soon as the new colonists began to feel the blessings of independence, they would rejoice that the legislature had opened to them a new scene of existence; they would find they had become valuable members of the community, and would in the end prove of essential service to the mother-country. The adoption of this plan would prove the means of restoring this country to a healthy state. The small note circulation, if allowed to take place, would make the agricultural interest flourish. The labouring classes would be happy and contented; and although they might not all be in the condition which the Lord Chancellor wished them to be in, when, in one of his speeches on education he is reported to have said, " that he looked forward to the day when every poor man in the kingdom should be able to read Bacon," still they would not have much reason to complain, if they all had it in their power, if not to read, yet to eat Bacon.

I am, my Lord,

Yours, &c.

E. N.

LONDON :

IBOTSON AND PALMER, PRINTERS, SAVOY STREET, STRAND.

www.ingramcontent.com/pod-product-compliance
Lightning Source LLC
Chambersburg PA
CBHW081307040426
42452CB00014B/2688